Weather

Wind

Snow

Scorpion

Fun

Duck

Rabb

Horse

Winter

Cat

Shell Seed

River · Nile

Frog

Rain

Cloud

H

Lightning

Planets Earth

Mars

Penguin

Flower

Plants

M

Facts

ouse

I0636165

This edition published by Parragon Books Ltd in 2014

Parragon Books Ltd
Chartist House
15–17 Trim Street
Bath BA1 1HA, UK
www.parragon.com

Written by Marcy Kelman. Vetted by Barbara Berliner, Fred Gerber – Director of Education Emeritus at the Queens Botanical
Gardens, the experts at Disney's Animal Kingdom Theme Park at Walt Disney World Resort and Dr Andrew Fraknoi.

Photos by: Photos.com, iStockphoto, Image Source, Photodisc, Comstock, Getty Images, Agephotostock, Corbis,
AP/Wideworld and NASA.gov

Pleiades © Robert Gendler
Io © NASA
Panda Cub © Zoo Atlanta

ISBN 978-1-4454-6545-6

Printed in China

My First
Encyclopedia

Discover the wonders of the world

PaRragon

Bath • New York • Singapore • Hong Kong • Cologne • Delhi
Melbourne • Amsterdam • Johannesburg • Shenzhen

A note for parents

This comprehensive encyclopedia is specially designed for inquisitive preschool children who are eager to learn about the planet they live on, the animals they share it with and the elements of nature that surround them.

- All the favourite Disney characters are on hand throughout the book to guide your child on an amazing journey of discovery.

- In the first chapter, the Disney characters share their sense of excitement and fun as they explore the animal world.

- In the second chapter, they introduce amazing facts about some incredible things found in nature.

- The final chapter contains fascinating information about the many wonders of Planet Earth.

- Why not set your child off on a learning adventure by introducing a fact a day? Each entry is numbered, so your child could learn a new fact every day for over 240 days!

What's inside?

Mammals

A mammal is a type of animal. There are more than 4,000 mammal species that live on Earth. You're a mammal, too!

▲ Mother cheetah lying with her cubs

How are mammals born?

Mammals grow inside their mothers until they are born. Most do not hatch from eggs, like birds or reptiles do.

What are mammals?

Mammals are warm-blooded animals, which means their bodies stay about the same temperature most of the time, regardless of their surroundings. Most mammals have hair or fur.

Black bear

▼ *Piglets feeding from their mother*

Baby mammal diet

Baby mammals drink milk from their mothers.

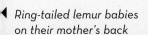
◀ *Ring-tailed lemur babies on their mother's back*

Dog

The dog is often called 'man's best friend'. That's because dogs are easy to train and they make loyal companions.

▼ Beagle

10

Fact 2

Most dogs make great family pets. But did you know that many dogs – such as police dogs – live and work side by side with humans?

◄ *Search-and-rescue dog*

Fact 3

Baby dogs are called puppies. Did you know that puppies cannot see or hear for the first two weeks of life? All puppies are born with blue eyes, but their eyes turn a permanent colour when they're about one month old.

West Highland terrier puppies ►

◄ *Jack Russell terrier*

Fact 4

Dogs can hear very high and very low noises that humans cannot. In fact, they can detect sounds that are four times farther away than humans are able to hear!

Rabbit

Rabbits live in many places, from swamps and woodlands to forests and deserts! Their long ears can turn in any direction to help them hear even the faintest sounds.

▼ Grey rabbit

Fact 6

Baby rabbits are called kits. Kits do not have fur when they are born, so they like to snuggle to stay warm and cosy in their burrows.

◀ *Kits in their burrow*

Rabbit standing on its hind legs ▶

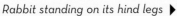

Fact 7

Rabbits thump their hind legs to let other rabbits know when they sense danger.

Fact 8

Rabbits usually live in groups in underground burrows. They eat grass, bark, leaves and berries.

◀ *Rabbit eating clover*

Elephant

Fact 13 There are two kinds of elephant: African elephants with very big ears and Asian elephants with smaller ears.

African elephant with her calf ▼

Fact 14 An elephant uses its trunk for breathing, smelling and picking up its favourite foods — such as hay, grasses and plant roots — and putting them in its mouth. To clean themselves, elephants suck water into their trunks and then hose themselves down.

▲ Elephant drinking from a water hole in South Africa

Fact 15 Baby elephants, which are called calves, sometimes use their trunks to hold on to their mothers' tails. Some calves put their trunks in their mouths to soothe themselves — just like human babies sucking their thumbs or dummies!

African elephant calf ▶

Fact 16 An elephant's wrinkly skin is very sensitive. Elephants usually roll around in mud and throw dirt on their backs to keep their skin cool and to protect it from sunburn and insect bites.

◀ Asian elephants playing in the mud

17

Chimpanzee

▲ Chimpanzee

Fact 17
Chimpanzees are our closest relatives in the animal world. They show their feelings very much the way humans do. They hug, kiss, smile and even hold on to each other when they're sad or scared. They also tickle each other when they're playing!

Fact 18
Unlike most animals, chimpanzees are able to make and use tools. They use rocks to crack open nuts and mash up fruit and they use sticks to catch ants and termites. Chimpanzees teach their young how to use tools for gathering food.

Chimpanzees sitting on a tree branch ▶

Fact 19
Chimpanzees have very long arms, which they use to swing from tree limbs and vines in the dense forests where they live.

◀ Chimpanzee in a tree

Kangaroo

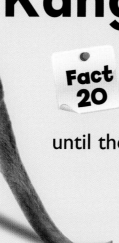

Fact 20

Kangaroos are marsupials — mammals that have pouches to carry around their babies until they are fully developed.

◀ *Young red kangaroo*

Fact 21

Baby kangaroos are called joeys. When they are born, joeys are about the size of a human thumb! A joey will feed and grow in its mother's pouch for almost one year.

Joey in its mother's pouch ▶

Fact 22

Other than low grunts or clucks, kangaroos don't make many noises — but they will thump their back feet to warn other kangaroos of danger. Kangaroos also use their tails for balance when standing, hopping or kicking.

◀ *Kangaroos in the Blue Mountains, New South Wales, Australia*

Panda

Fact 23 Pandas are bears with black-and-white fur coats. Most of a panda's body is white, but its arms, legs, ears and eye patches are usually black. Pandas can only be found living in the wild in one place: China.

Pandas have black-and-white fur, like me!

A panda eating ▼

Fact 24

In China, pandas can be found living in rainy bamboo forests, high in the mountains. Unlike other bears, which primarily eat meat, the panda is a plant eater that lives on a diet of bamboo shoots and leaves.

◄ Panda gets a drink

Fact 25

When panda cubs are born, all of their fur is white. Their black spots start to develop when they're one month old. Mother pandas like to wrestle and play with their young cubs.

Mother panda with her cub ►

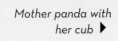

Fact 26

Giant pandas have enlarged wrist bones on their front paws that act like human thumbs. These 'thumbs' help them to hold and eat bamboo – their favourite food.

◄ Panda munching on bamboo

Lion

Fact 27 Lions are members of the cat family. They live on the savannah in groups of 15 to 40 lions. These groups are called prides.

Two lion cubs hiding under a bush ▼

Fact 28

Lions are the only cats with tufts of hair at the end of their tails. The male lions also have manes around their necks. Is the lion in this picture male or female?

◀ African lion

Fact 29

In addition to taking turns to babysit and nurse each other's cubs, lionesses usually hunt together as a team to feed the whole pride.

A lioness cuddling with her young cub ▶

Fact 30

Lions can roar louder than other big cats, such as the leopard, tiger or jaguar. A lion's roar can be heard up to eight kilometres away! Most lions don't start roaring until they are about two years old.

◀ A lion roaring

Flying eagle owl ▶

▼ *Sparrows in a nest*

Birds

Birds can caw, coo, sing or chirp. Some birds can even repeat words that they hear people say!

How are birds born?

Every bird hatches from an egg.

◀ *Toucan*

24

What are birds?

All birds are animals with wings and feathers, but not all birds can fly. Some just swim or walk.

How do birds eat?

Birds don't have teeth. They use their sharp beaks to 'chew' their food.

Peacock fanning its feathers ▶

Hummingbird

Anna's hummingbird

Fact 31

Hummingbirds are the smallest birds in the world. The tiniest hummingbird, called the bee hummingbird, is only 6 centimetres long!

Fact 32

The hummingbird can rotate its wings in a circle, making it the only bird that is able to fly upwards, downwards, forwards, backwards and sideways. They fly at an average speed of 48 kilometres per hour.

Hummingbird feeding on a flower ▶

Fact 33

Living in forests and meadows, hummingbirds fly from flower to flower, using their long, pointed beaks to sip nectar. Hummingbirds often collect nectar from as many as one thousand flowers in one day!

◀ *Ruby-throated hummingbird*

Ostrich

Fact 34

The ostrich is the largest bird in the world. Although it cannot fly, the ostrich can run at about 65 kilometres per hour – faster than any other bird!

◀ Ostriches have big eyes

Fact 35

One ostrich egg is about the size of 24 chicken eggs! Ostrich chicks are already 30 centimetres tall when they're born. Adult ostriches can grow to be a metre taller than most grown-up people!

Ostrich chick ▶

Fact 36

If an ostrich feels threatened, it kicks. Ostriches use their strong and powerful kick to protect themselves against animals such as lions.

◀ Ostrich

Penguin

Fact 37

Most penguins are black and white. They are birds that live in the cool waters south of the equator.

King penguins at the beach in the rain ▼

Fact 38

A group of penguins living together is called a rookery. Living side by side with many other penguins allows them to huddle together and stay warm.

◀ King penguins

Gentoo penguins ▶

Fact 39

Penguins are excellent swimmers, but they cannot fly. They use their flippers to paddle through the water and to keep their balance when waddling across slippery surfaces such as wet rocks or ice.

Fact 40

Usually, female penguins lay one egg at a time. Male and female penguins take it in turns to look after the egg. A female penguin will often go hunting for food while the male keeps the egg warm.

◀ A penguin looking after an egg

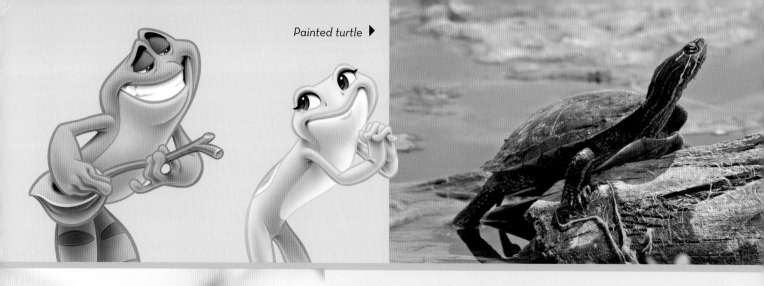

Painted turtle ▶

Reptiles and amphibians

Both reptiles and amphibians are cold-blooded. This means that their bodies are the same temperature as their surroundings.

▲ A green tree python hatching

Born or hatched?

Most reptiles and amphibians hatch from eggs. But amphibian eggs do not have a hard, protective shell like reptile or bird eggs do.

◀ Green iguana

What are reptiles?

Reptiles are animals that are covered with scales. Scales are rough, dry pieces of skin that protect a reptile's body.

What are amphibians?

Red-eyed tree frog ▶

Amphibians are animals that don't have hair, fur, feathers or scales. They have wet, smooth skin. Most amphibians live in or around water because they must keep their skin moist.

Chameleon

Chameleons are lizards that can change the shade of their skin to almost any colour in the rainbow. Scientists believe that they change their colour based on their mood or in reaction to changes in light and temperature.

Jackson's chameleon ▼

Fact 42

Chameleons can turn their eyes separately in any direction. They can look behind them without turning their heads and can even look forwards with one eye and backwards with the other!

◀ *Chameleon hidden amongst leaves*

Fact 43

Chameleons are one of the few lizards that have a prehensile, or grasping, tail. They wrap their special tails around branches as they climb trees.

Chameleon showing its long tail ▲

Fact 44

Chameleons have long, sticky tongues that they can quickly flick in the air to catch insects. Their tongues are sometimes twice the length of their bodies!

◀ *This baby veiled chameleon is picking up a fly with its tongue*

Giant tortoise

Fact 45
The giant tortoise is one of the longest-living animals on Earth. Many of them live for more than 150 years! The giant tortoise can grow to be longer than a metre and a half, and can weigh over 200 kilograms.

◀ *Giant tortoise*

Fact 46
To rid themselves of ticks and other bugs, giant tortoises get some help from birds. The tortoise will raise itself up on its legs and stretch out its neck to invite birds to rest on its head and remove any pests that might be on its body.

Giant tortoise ▶

Fact 47
If a tortoise senses danger, it will hide its head, neck and legs inside its hard shell. Unlike turtles, tortoises spend their lives on land. They eat shrubs, grasses and even cacti.

◀ *Galapagos giant tortoise*

Poison dart frog

Fact 48
The poison dart frog is an amphibian. They capture spiders, ants and termites with their long, sticky tongues. Poison dart frogs are often less than 2 centimetres long, but they can grow to over 6 centimetres!

◀ *Blue-and-black poison dart frog*

Fact 49
Unlike other frogs, the male poison dart frog cares for his babies by watching over the eggs. Once they hatch, tadpoles swim onto the dad's back, and then he carries them to a safe spot where they can continue to grow.

Orange-and-black poison dart frog ▶

Fact 50
The poison dart frog – also called the poison arrow frog – got its name from native South American tribes, who used the poison from the frogs' skin on the tips of their blowgun darts.

◀ *Peruvian poison dart frog*

I live in the sea!

Orca ▼

Sea creatures

Sea creatures are animals that live in or around the sea.

What are sea mammals?

Some sea creatures are mammals. Sea mammals can't stay underwater all the time. They have to come to the surface to breathe air.

California sea lions ▼

What are fish?

Fish are creatures that live in the water and have gills to help them breathe. Most fish have fins to help them swim.

◀ *A fish under the sea*

What other animals live in the sea?

Other sea creatures, such as crabs and lobsters, have shells, long arms or sharp claws and stay underwater most of the time.

Sally Lightfoot crab ▶

Dolphin

Fact 51 Dolphins are sea mammals, which means that they live in the water but must come to the surface to breathe.

Dolphins usually sleep with one eye open!

Bottlenose dolphin ▼

Fact 52 Like Marlin and Nemo, dolphins live with their family. They stay together in family groups of 10 or 12 dolphins. These groups are called pods.

◄ *A pod of dolphins*

Fact 53 As soon as baby dolphins are born, they swim up to the surface to breathe air and then return to drink their mothers' milk. Baby dolphins stay with their mothers for three to six years before joining a pod of other young dolphins.

A mother dolphin jumping out of the water with her calf ►

Fact 54 Dolphins are friendly, playful animals that are very close to other members of their pods. If a dolphin is having trouble breathing, the other dolphins in the pod will work together to help it reach the surface so that it can get air.

◄ *A baby Atlantic bottlenose dolphin with its mother*

Shark

Fact 55 Sharks are fish that have been on Earth for a very long time. In fact, they were around 100 million years before dinosaurs lived!

◄ Great white shark

Hammerhead shark ►

Fact 56 Unlike other fish, sharks do not have bones. Sharks' skeletons are made of cartilage — the same stuff that our noses and ears are made from. Sharks, however, do have sharp, bony teeth. If a tooth is damaged or lost, a shark can grow a new one. A typical shark has about 30,000 teeth throughout its lifetime.

▼ Zebra shark

Fact 57 There are many kinds of shark. Some grow to be the length of a pencil, while others can grow to weigh as much as two elephants! Most sharks, though, are the size of people.

Octopus

Fact 58
The name octopus means 'eight feet'. Each of its eight arms has two rows of suction cups, which help it pry open shells. If the octopus loses one of its arms, it can grow a new one!

▲ Young octopus

Fact 59

The octopus uses its arms to catch crabs, fish, turtles, shrimp and other octopuses. It then uses its parrot-like beak to inject a venom into its prey.

Octopus gliding through the water ▶

Fact 60
Octopuses move along the bottom of the ocean by walking on their arms, gripping the ocean floor with their suction cups. To move quickly through the water, octopuses use jet propulsion: they expel water from their bodies to move themselves along.

◀ Red octopus

Honeybee ▶

Bugs and cool crawlers

Most bugs and cool crawlers have exoskeletons, which means their skeletons are on the outside of their bodies.

Spider ▲

What are arachnids?

Arachnids are animals with eight legs, such as spiders, scorpions and ticks.

Stag beetle ▶

What are insects?

Insects are animals with six legs. Many of them have wings and antennae.

We're going to learn about insects, arachnids and other cool crawlers!

Red-coloured millipede ▶

Other crawlers

There are also plenty of animals that don't have six or eight legs. Millipedes and centipedes have between 30 and 200 legs, worms have no legs and snails have one big leg called a foot.

Tarantula

Fact 61

The world's biggest — and hairiest — spider is the tarantula. While some are as small as a bottle cap, the largest ones can be as big as a dinner plate!

Roooaar! I'm scarier than a spider!

Mexican red knee tarantula ▼

Fact 62

Tarantulas live in warm climates such as hot, dry deserts or humid rainforests. Most live in burrows in the ground, but some live in trees.

◀ Tarantula

Fact 63

Tarantulas from North and South America have a great way of annoying their enemies – they have hairs on their backs that they can rub off using their back legs. These hairs stick to other animals and make them very itchy!

Red knee tarantula ▲

Fact 64

Tarantulas are venomous, but their venom won't seriously harm humans. If a tarantula were to bite a human, the effect would be no worse than a bee sting.

◀ A woman holding a tarantula

Scorpion

Fact 65

Just like spiders and ticks, scorpions are members of the arachnid family. They have tiny hooks at the end of each of their eight legs.

No scorpion is as scary as me!

Emperor scorpion ▼

Fact 66

A scorpion has two pincers near its head and a curved tail with a venomous stinger on the end.

◀ *Emperor scorpion*

Fact 67

Many scorpions are found in warm, dry areas, such as the desert, where tracking down food and water can be difficult. Scorpions usually eat insects, lizards and rodents, but if food is hard to find, they can survive on just a few meals a year!

Scorpion in a defensive position ▶

Fact 68

Baby scorpions are born bright white! Adult scorpions are black, brown or reddish-black. A mother scorpion carries her babies on her back for several weeks.

◀ *Baby scorpions*

Caterpillar

Fact 69
A caterpillar is a baby butterfly or moth. Most caterpillars have 16 legs and spend most of their time eating leaves and flowers. As it eats, a caterpillar gets bigger and bigger.

◀ Caterpillar

Fact 70
When we grow, our skin grows with us – but did you know that a caterpillar's skin doesn't grow with it? As a caterpillar grows, it needs to shed its skin. This is called moulting. Caterpillars shed their skin four or five times before becoming adults.

Caterpillar ▶

Fact 71
A caterpillar has a strong mouth and jaws to help it eat leaves. It grows as it eats, until its hard skin becomes a chrysalis. Then it stays inside the chrysalis until it turns into a butterfly.

◀ Chrysalis of a monarch butterfly

Butterfly

Fact 72 Some butterflies have brightly coloured wings as a warning to predators that they taste bad! Some butterflies have dull-coloured wings for good camouflage.

Fact 73 Butterflies do not have mouths to bite into food. Instead, they drink flower nectar through a straw-like tube called a proboscis, which looks like a long, black tongue.

Blue Salamis butterfly ▶

Fact 74 Butterflies smell with their antennae and breathe through tiny holes along the sides of their bodies. They also use their feet to taste food! Butterflies have special sensors on their feet that let them 'taste' the flower or fruit they're standing on.

◀ *Monarch butterfly*

Fun facts!

They may be considered among the scariest-looking animals on the planet, but these featured creatures are truly amazing members of the animal kingdom! Here are some frightfully fun facts about them.

A female black widow spider has a red or orange 'hourglass' shape on her belly.

Bat

FACT 75 Even though bats have wings, they are not birds. Bats are mammals, just like humans. The bones in their wings are similar to those in our arms and hands, and they even have small, thumb-like claws on their wings to grasp things.

Black widow spider

FACT 76 Most spiders make spiderwebs. They build them from silk. The black widow's silk is stronger than that of almost any other spider.

Cockroach

FACT 77 Cockroaches are tough insects. They can live without food for a month and can live without their heads for about a week!

Jellyfish

FACT 78 Jellyfish don't have eyes, ears, a brain or even a heart! Even so, they are able to capture food by using their long, poisonous tentacles to sting fish.

Kiwi

FACT 79 Kiwis are birds that live in New Zealand. They are about the size of a chicken and have long beaks and no tails. Kiwis' wings are only 5 centimetres long, so it's no wonder they can't fly!

Anaconda

FACT 80 Anacondas can be found in the swamps, lakes and rivers of South America. They are the largest snakes in the world. Anacondas can grow to be six metres long and can weigh up to 140 kilograms!

Snail

FACT 81 It looks as though snails crawl along on their bellies, but the bottom part of a snail is really its foot.

Sloth

FACT 82 Sloths are known for being the world's slowest animals! They live in the rainforest and sleep for 20 hours a day.

Turkey

FACT 83 Each turkey has a fleshy wattle under its beak and a fleshy flap of skin called a snood that hangs over its beak. Both turn bright red when the turkey gets upset!

◀ *Autumn leaves*

Seasons

A season is a period of time during the year. There are four seasons in one year: spring, summer, autumn and winter.

▲ *Autumn sunshine*

Seasons around the world

When it is summer in one part of the world, it could be winter in another!

▼ *Crocus flowering in winter*

How long is a season?

Each season is about three months long. The seasons change slowly, going from spring to summer to autumn to winter and back to spring again.

▼ Grapes

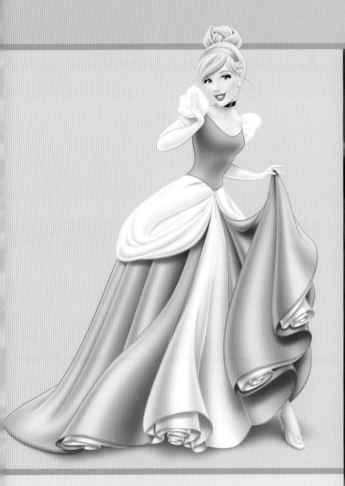

Seasons change

In some parts of the world, the weather changes when the seasons change. The types of plants that bloom and the behaviour of animals can also change from one season to the next.

Spring

Fact 84

In some parts of the world, the weather gets warmer when spring arrives, helping to melt away winter's snow and ice.

When spring arrives, there is lots of food to eat in the forest!

▼ *Girl blowing dandelion seeds*

Fact 85

In spring, the days grow longer, which means it stays light outside later into the evening.

◀ *Evening sunshine in a forest*

Fact 86

In spring, many flowers start blooming. Trees that have rested all winter begin growing leaves and their buds begin to open. Spring often brings lots of rainy days, which are good for helping plants to grow.

Wild blue crocuses blooming ▶

Fact 87

Birds, frogs and many other animals are born in spring. It's also a busy time for bees, which fly from flower to flower collecting the nectar they need to make honey.

◀ *Honeybee gathering nectar*

55

Summer

Fact 88 In some parts of the world, summer arrives in late June and it's hot and sunny outdoors. The days grow even longer than the days in spring. In some places, it stays light outside all through the night!

Summer in the savannah is hot, hot, hot!

▼ Girl on the beach in summer

In the summer, many trees are covered with big, green leaves, providing us with shade from the Sun. Grass grows tall at this time of year and the sweet smells of roses, lilies and other summer flowers often fill the air.

Bees and butterflies land on the flowers of fruit and vegetable plants to collect nectar. The insects spread pollen, which helps the flowers grow into tasty summer fruits with seeds that will grow into new plants.

Monarch butterflies ▶

During the hot summer months, insects such as ladybirds, wasps and mosquitoes can be seen flying here and there. Have you ever seen a ladybird where you live?

◀ *Ladybird*

Autumn

Fact 92 In autumn, the weather gets cooler and the Sun sets earlier in the day.

Bouncing in crunchy autumn leaves is what Tiggers do best!

▼ Boy collecting autumn leaves

Fact 93

When the days get shorter and it begins to get chilly outside, some animals know that it's time to start gathering nuts and berries to eat during the cold winter months.

◀ *Squirrel*

Fact 94

In some places, leaves start to change colour in autumn, becoming red, yellow or orange. As the weather gets even colder, these leaves will fall from the trees and turn brown and crispy.

Autumn leaves by a river ▶

Fact 95

Many delicious fruits and vegetables – such as apples, pears, pumpkins, lettuce, cabbage, grapes, chestnuts, turnips and broccoli – are ready to be picked in autumn.

◀ *Apple tree*

Winter

Fact 96

By the time winter arrives in some parts of the world, autumn's colourful leaves have fallen and the trees are bare. During winter, frost often appears on the grass in the morning.

Snowman ▼

We love making snowmen in winter!

Fact 97

In many places, winter is the coldest time of the year. It can get very windy, snowy and icy outside. Ponds and lakes may freeze and turn to ice.

◀ *A street covered with snow*

Fact 98

Winter days are very short. The Sun sets early in the evening and, without the Sun's light to warm the air, the temperature gets colder.

Winter sun setting ▶

Fact 99

Some animals change their appearance in winter. This weasel's brown coat turns white in winter. The white fur helps it blend in with snow and stay hidden from predators. In spring, the weasel will shed its white coat and have a brown one again.

◀ *Weasel*

Snow on trees ▲

Weather

When we talk about weather, we're talking about what the air is like in a certain area. Is the air hot and dry? Is it cold and damp?

Changes in the weather

Weather is always changing. It changes from hour to hour and day to day. People who study the weather are called meteorologists. A barometer, such as this one, is one instrument used to predict the weather.

Barometer ▶

What is weather?

Weather is made up of different things, such as wind, temperature, sunshine and clouds.

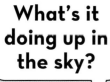

What's it doing up in the sky?

It looks as though the weather can't make up its mind!

What affects the weather?

Water in the air affects the weather. Without water, there could be no clouds, rain, lightning or snow!

Lightning strikes ▶

Cloud

Fact 100 Clouds are formed from water in the air that you can't see. This 'invisible water' is called water vapour. When water vapour rises high into the sky, where it is very cold, the vapour forms a cloud!

Flying through the clouds is wonderful!

Clouds ▼

Fact 101

Some clouds look like big puffs of cotton. These are called cumulus clouds. Cirrus clouds are thin and curly, while stratus clouds look like long, flat layers of white. Without looking at the label, can you tell what type of clouds are in this picture?

◄ *Cumulus clouds*

Fact 102

Dark grey clouds are called nimbus clouds. When you see nimbus clouds filling the sky and making it dark, it means it's ready to rain. Nimbus means 'rainstorm' in Latin, which is why these clouds are also called rain clouds.

Nimbus clouds ►

Fact 103

A cumulonimbus cloud is a large, dark and puffy cloud that's electrically charged. Its name is a combination of the words cumulus and nimbus. Cumulonimbus clouds are better known as thunderclouds!

◄ *Cumulonimbus clouds*

Rain

Fact 104 Rain forms when the vapour that forms clouds turns into droplets of water and falls from the sky.

Pouring rain ▼

Fact 105

Raindrops can come down in a gentle sprinkle, or in heavy sheets that sometimes cause leaves and flowers to break off from their stems.

◀ *Raindrops on grass*

Fact 106

Rain soaks into the ground, giving trees, grass, flowers, fruits and vegetables the water they need to grow.

Spring flowers in the rain ▶

Fact 107

Some rain soaks deep into the earth. Humans use wells and underground pipes to bring that rainwater up out of the ground to use in their homes. This is some of the water that comes out of our taps!

◀ *Old-fashioned water pump*

Lightning

Fact 108 There are millions of water droplets in rain clouds. During a storm, the activity of the droplets rubbing against each other creates electricity. This is called lightning!

Wow, cool!

Lightning bolts ▼

Fact 109

Every second of every day, there are 50 to 100 instances of lightning striking the ground somewhere in the world!

◀ *Summer lightning storm*

Fact 110

The temperature of a lightning bolt is hotter than the temperature of the Sun! Since lightning heats the air so quickly, a bolt makes the cold air around it shake with a loud sound, called thunder. Have you ever heard thunder during a storm?

A thunderstorm moving across the open country ▶

Fact 111

If you listen closely to the sound of thunder, you can tell how close the lightning is. If it's far away, you may hear a low rumble or no sound at all. But the closer the lightning gets, the louder the crackle or bang it makes!

◀ *A powerful lightning bolt*

Snow

Fact 112 In cold temperatures, clouds will form ice crystals instead of raindrops. These crystals become heavy and fall to the ground as snow.

Snowman ▼

Fact 113

All snowflakes have six sides, but no two snowflakes look exactly alike. When it's very cold out, snowflakes are small, long and thin. When it's slightly warmer, they're larger and have more detailed designs.

◀ *Magnified snowflake*

Fact 114

Snowflakes begin as ice crystals that are as small as specks of dust. As they fall, the crystals connect to other crystals and form snowflakes. Some snowflakes look like flowers, stars, spiderwebs or even lightning bolts.

'Snow Angel' shape made by a child in the snow ▶

Fact 115

In the Arctic, people on fishing or hunting trips may build shelters made of snow. These shelters are called igloos. Even though they're made using big blocks of snow, igloos keep people warm by keeping hot air trapped inside and the cold air outside.

◀ *Igloo made from blocks of snow*

Wind

Fact 116
Although you can't see the wind, you can feel it moving through the air. Wind can be very strong and powerful, making leaves and kites – or even hundreds of balloons – lift into the air. Or it can feel like a soft, gentle whisper against your skin.

Boats using the wind to sail ▼

Wind turbines

Fact 117 Sometimes we use the wind's energy to make machines and vehicles move. Windmills are farm machines that use the wind's energy to collect water or grind up grain, while sailing boats use the wind's force to glide across the water.

Fact 118 The wind carries plants' seeds from one place to another. Wherever the seeds fall, they have a chance to grow into new plants. Many of the flowers and plants you see may have grown from seeds that were blown there from far away.

Dandelion ▶

◀ Kitesurfers

Fact 119 Some people use the wind to do fun water sports, like kitesurfing! A popular place for water sports is on the southern coast of Spain, where a narrow stretch of water called the Strait of Gibraltar forms a perfect wind tunnel between Spain and Africa.

Children fishing by a river ▼

Bodies of water

Water is everywhere. People drink it, fish live in it and birds bathe in it.

What is saltwater?

The water found in the ocean is saltwater. Lobsters, whales, dolphins, clams and starfish are just a few of the animals found living in the ocean's saltwater.

Starfish ▲

Lobster ▶

Water, water everywhere

Water drips, flows and splashes. It can be forceful, like a fast-moving river, or calm and silent, like a lake.

Every living thing needs water to grow.

Fish, like me, live in the water!

What is freshwater?

The water in lakes, ponds, rivers, streams, marshes and swamps is called freshwater. Many different fish, reptiles and amphibians live in freshwater.

Trout ▶

Lake and pond

A lake is a large body of water surrounded by land. Some lakes are very deep. Ponds are smaller than lakes and aren't as deep.

I live in the bayou – that's a marshy type of lake!

Canada ▼

Fact 121

Lakes and ponds are home to many interesting plants and animals. You can find frogs, beavers, ducks, turtles, snakes, reeds and flowering lily pads living in or around lakes and ponds.

◀ *Ducklings*

Elk cooling in a lake ▶

Fact 122

Unlike the ocean, the water in lakes isn't constantly moving and crashing as waves; it's actually very smooth. The wind, however, can create tiny waves that are called ripples.

Lake Baikal, Siberia ▼

Fact 123

Lake Baikal in Siberia is the world's deepest lake and oldest lake. It is 1.6 kilometres deep and around 25 million years old! Lake Baikal is also home to the world's only freshwater seals.

River and stream

Lots of friendly creatures live in rivers and streams!

Fact 124

Rivers are wide, long bodies of flowing freshwater. Streams are shorter and narrower than rivers.

Bridges over a large river ▼

Fact 125

Rivers and streams don't flow in a straight line. They twist and turn as they flow. Rivers start in the mountains or hills and usually end up flowing into a large body of water, such as an ocean, bay or sea.

◀ Curvy river

Fact 126

Rivers can be deep and fast moving or shallow and slow. Some rivers are muddy and brownish, while others are crystal clear.

River valley ▶

Fact 127

The Nile is the longest river in the world. It is about 6,650 kilometres long! Located in Africa, the Nile flows through nine countries and out into the Mediterranean Sea.

◀ Boats on the River Nile

Ocean

Today's a perfect day for the beach!

Fact 128 Oceans are very large bodies of water. When you go to the beach, you can see the ocean waves rolling in and out, crashing against the seashore. Have you ever tasted ocean water at the beach? It is very salty!

Beach ▼

Fact 129

There are five oceans in the world: the Arctic, Atlantic, Indian, Pacific and Southern. The Pacific Ocean is the biggest ocean in the world. In fact, it covers around 30 per cent of the Earth's surface.

◀ *The Great Barrier Reef in Australia*

Fact 130

Ocean waves are caused by gusts of wind. The size and strength of waves depend on how fast the wind is blowing, where it's blowing from and for how long it's been blowing.

Wave ▶

Fact 131

Swells are stable and constant waves that have been created by storms. Swells may travel thousands of kilometres before they finally reach land! Swells are the waves that surfers love to ride.

◀ *Surfer*

Glacier and iceberg

Glaciers contain more ice than the whole of Pixie Hollow's Winter Woods!

Fact 132

Glaciers are like huge slow-moving rivers of ice. Icebergs are enormous chunks of ice floating in the ocean.

Dawes Glacier, Alaska, USA ▼

Fact 133

Glaciers can be hundreds of kilometres long, while icebergs are often as big as mountains. Icebergs are even bigger than they look, because more than half of an iceberg is hidden under the water!

◀ *Icebergs*

Icebergs from the Vatnajokull glacier in Iceland ▶

Fact 134

Icebergs are often found in the oceans around the North and South Pole regions, where it is very cold. They break away from glaciers and ice shelves and drift away.

Fact 135

When icebergs reach warmer waters, they start to melt, crack and break up. This process can be very, very noisy!

◀ *Seals resting on a floating piece of ice*

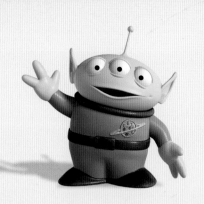

Space

We call the area outside the Earth's atmosphere 'space'.

◀ Saturn

What are planets?

Very far away, high up in the sky are big, round objects called planets. There are eight planets in the solar system, including our planet, Earth.

Jupiter ▶

Where are planets?

The Sun, Moon, planets and stars are very far away from us. We call the place where they're found 'outer space'.

To infinity and beyond!

How do we learn about planets?

Scientists who study outer space are called astronomers. They use powerful telescopes to help them see faraway objects such as planets and stars.

◀ *Model of the Hubble telescope*

Solar system

'Solar' means belonging to the Sun. The Sun is at the centre of the Earth's solar system.

Think, think, think! Can you find Earth on this map of the solar system?

Our solar system ▼

Fact 137 Our solar system includes the Sun and the planets that travel around it. What else can you find floating around our solar system? About 400,000 asteroids! They are pieces of rock left over from the formation of the solar system nearly 4.5 billion years ago.

◄ *View of space*

Fact 138 Earth, the planet we live on, is one of eight planets that travel around the Sun. The other seven planets are Mercury, Venus, Mars, Jupiter, Saturn, Uranus and Neptune. Some planets have moons, too, such as Jupiter, shown here with four of its moons.

Jupiter and its moons ▶

Fact 139

Each planet takes a different amount of time to circle around the Sun. It takes one year for the Earth to travel around the Sun once, with each year lasting 365 days.

◄ *Sun, Earth and our Moon*

Earth

Fact 140 We all live on the planet called Earth. It is the only planet we know of with people and animals living on it.

The Earth travels around the Sun ▼

Fact 141

Although you can't feel it, the Earth is constantly spinning. At the equator, the Earth spins at around 1,670 kilometres per hour. It takes 24 hours (a whole day) for the Earth to spin around once.

◀ *View of Earth from space*

Fact 142

As the Earth is spinning, or rotating, it's also making its long, 365-day trip around the Sun. Believe it or not, the Earth moves at a speed of 30 kilometres per second!

The international space station ▶

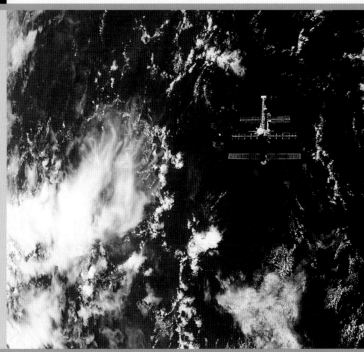

Fact 143

Earth is often called the 'Blue Planet' because of all the water that covers it. Our oceans cover almost three quarters of the Earth's surface.

◀ *Earth*

Sun

Fact 144 Did you know that the Sun is a star, just like the ones we see in the night sky? The Sun is much closer to Earth than any other stars, so it looks much bigger and brighter. The Sun is close enough to Earth for us to feel its warmth.

Golden sunset ▼

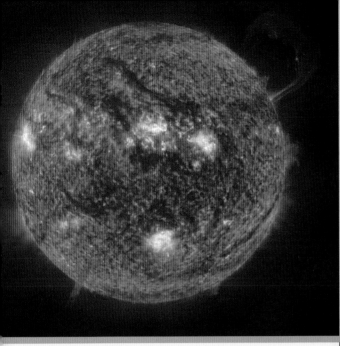

Fact 145

Without the Sun, there wouldn't be any life on Earth; our planet would be dark and frozen and wouldn't have any plants or animals. Like all living things, humans need the Sun's light, heat and energy to survive and grow.

◄ *Solar flare*

Fact 146

Although it looks small in the sky, the Sun is actually much bigger than Earth. In fact, the Sun is about a million times bigger than the Earth. If the Earth were the size of a pinhead, the Sun would be the size of a football!

Earth with the rising Sun ►

Fact 147

As Earth rotates around the Sun, different areas of the planet feel the Sun's heat more than others. Some places are experiencing winter, while others are going through the summer season. What season is it now in your part of the world?

◄ *Sunset*

Moon

Fact 148

When you see the Moon at night, it seems to be shining, but the Moon doesn't give off any light of its own. It is actually a dull grey colour, but it looks bright white to us because it reflects light from the Sun.

Shoot! Lightning told me the Moon changes shape. What does it look like outta your window tonight?

Nighttime sky in a forest ▼

Fact 149

As the Moon travels around the Earth, the Sun shines on it at different angles, changing the way the Moon looks in the sky. It might look like a circle, a semicircle or even a crescent.

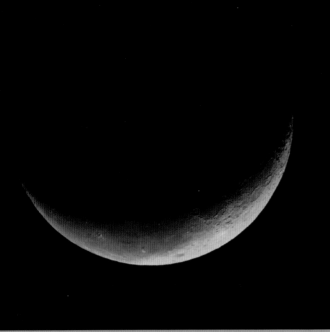

◀ Crescent moon

Surface of the Moon ▶

Fact 150

The surface of the Moon has many deep holes, called craters. When viewed from Earth, the biggest craters make a dark pattern that almost looks like a face on the Moon. Can you see the 'face' on the Moon?

Fact 151

Six of the eight planets in our solar system have one or more moons. Earth has one, Mars has two, Neptune has 14, Uranus has 27 and Saturn has 62. Jupiter has 67 that we know of, and new ones are being discovered all the time.

◀ Io, a moon of Jupiter

93

Fun facts!

Climb aboard and get ready to explore! Buzz Lightyear and Woody are taking a trip through the solar system. They've got some fascinating facts about the planets that are simply out of this world!

Mercury and Venus are the only two planets in the solar system that don't have moons orbiting them. The planet with the most moons is Jupiter.

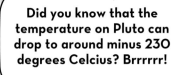

Did you know that the temperature on Pluto can drop to around minus 230 degrees Celcius? Brrrrrr!

Mercury

FACT 152 Mercury is the closest planet to the Sun, even though it is still about 58 million kilometres away! Mercury travels around the Sun faster than any other planet in our solar system.

FACT 153 Mercury looks a lot like our moon. It's very rocky and has lots of craters, but it's a little bit bigger than our moon.

Venus

FACT 154 Venus is the only planet in the solar system that spins in the opposite direction to Earth. It also spins very slowly.

FACT 155 Venus has more volcanoes than any other planet in the solar system. Scientists are not sure if the volcanoes are inactive or if they'll erupt in the future.

Mars

FACT 156 Mars is called the 'Red Planet' because of its rocky, orange-red soil. Known for its many dust storms, the sky on Mars always looks pink or pale orange in colour.

FACT 157 Mars has two moons, which are not round in shape and are much smaller than Earth's moon. Phobos is only 18 kilometres wide, while Deimos is around 12 kilometres wide!

Jupiter

FACT 158 Jupiter is the largest planet in the solar system. It's so big that 1,300 Earths could fit inside it!

FACT 159 Jupiter has a 'Great Red Spot', which is actually a huge, hurricane-like storm with winds of up to 400 kilometres per hour.

Saturn

FACT 160 Saturn is a large planet known for its hundreds of colourful rings. The rings are actually made up of ice, dust and bits of rock.

FACT 161 The planet Saturn takes about 30 Earth years to revolve around the Sun. It travels at almost 35,000 kilometres per hour!

Uranus

FACT 162 Uranus is the third-largest planet in the solar system. About 63 Earths could fit inside Uranus.

FACT 163 Uranus is surrounded by 27 grey moons.

Neptune

FACT 164 Of all the planets, Neptune has the craziest weather. It has really big storms with very fast winds, some of which have reached more than 1,000 kilometres per hour!

FACT 165 Due to its deep blue colour, the planet Neptune was named after the Roman god of the sea. Neptune has 13 moons.

Pluto

FACT 166 Beginning in 1930, Pluto was considered to be the ninth planet in our solar system. But due to its small size and irregular orbit, astronomers decided to classify it as a 'dwarf planet' in 2006.

FACT 167 It takes Pluto about 248 Earth years to orbit around the Sun once.

Plants

Trees, grass and flowers are all plants. Fruits, vegetables and leaves all come from plants.

Corn growing in summer ▲

What do plants look like?

Plants come in many different colours, shapes and sizes. A plant can be as tiny as your fingertip or as tall as a house!

Sunflower ▶

What are plants?

Most plants have roots, stems and seeds.
Nearly all plants have leaves.

What makes plants grow?

All plants need light, water and air to grow. Plants are the main source of oxygen production on Earth, since they release more oxygen back into the air than they use.

Potted and hanging plants ▶

Seed

Fact 168

Most plants, from tall trees to tiny flowers, start off as seeds. Seeds grow in the soil. First they sprout roots, which grow downwards and anchor the seeds in the soil.

Have you ever blown dandelion seeds into the air?

Rice plant ▼

◀ *Seedling poking out of the soil*

Fact 169

Then, after getting plenty of water and warmth, a little stem starts to poke out of the top of the seed, pushing its way up and out of the soil. Soon the stem may grow leaves and become a big plant!

Watermelon ▶

Fact 170

When you cut into certain fruits, such as cucumbers, watermelons, tomatoes and apples, you can see their tiny seeds inside!

Fact 171

Have you ever seen squirrels gathering acorns? Acorns are actually the seeds of oak trees! All oak trees begin as little acorns.

◀ *Acorns*

Flower

Fact 172

Flowers are the pretty blossoms on plants. They come in many colours, shapes and sizes. They grow in the woods and in gardens, fields and parks.

Wet tulips ▼

Fact 173

The sunflower is one of the tallest flowers in the world. Some have grown to be more than 7 metres tall! Tiny seeds grow in the middle of sunflowers. Have you ever eaten sunflower seeds?

◀ Sunflowers

Fact 174

Many flowers, such as roses, lilacs and lilies, smell very sweet. Bees, hummingbirds and butterflies are attracted to the colour and smell of flowers and drink their sweet nectar.

Monarch butterfly ▶

Fact 175

The stinkiest flower in the world is the rafflesia flower. It attracts a lot of flies because it smells like rotting meat!

◀ Rafflesia flower

Grass

Grass grows in places such as parks, gardens and fields. There are more than 10,000 types of grass! Grass isn't always green – it comes in a variety of colours, sizes and textures.

Dune grass ▼

Fact 177

A lot of the foods you eat, such as oats, rice and wheat, are grasses. Even some of our sugar comes from the stem of a grass called sugarcane.

◀ *Golden wheat*

Fact 178

Many animals, such as cows, horses and sheep, eat grass. Grass can also be woven into baskets and is used in some countries to make roofs for houses.

Children sitting in grass ▶

Fact 179

Bamboo is the tallest grass in the world. It grows very fast. In fact, it can grow as much as 30 centimetres in one day!

◀ *Bamboo*

Tree

Fact 180

There are two types of trees: deciduous and evergreen. The leaves of deciduous trees start growing in spring, change colour in autumn and drop off in winter. Evergreen trees, such as pine trees, keep their leaves all year.

I'm made of wood that came from a tree!

Changing leaves on trees ▼

Fact 181

Trees are homes for many animals. Some animals build their nests on tree branches; others live in holes in trees or sleep in hollow logs that have fallen on the ground.

◀ *Bald eagle in its nest*

Fact 182 The wood from trees can be used to build houses, boats, fences and furniture. Most of the paper we use – from newspapers and books to cardboard boxes and toilet paper – comes from trees!

A house being built from wood ▶

Fact 183 You can look at a slice of a tree trunk and count the rings to determine how old the tree is – one ring equals one year!

◀ *Rings of a tree trunk*

Garden

Fact 184

A garden is an area, usually outdoors, where people plant and grow plants.

Pretty flowers all in rows, this is how my garden grows!

Garden ▼

You don't need a large area to grow a garden. In fact, many people plant gardens in pots or window boxes.

◀ *Window box*

Fact 186

A garden can have fruits, vegetables, flowers or all of these kinds of plants growing together. Gardens need sun, water and lots of care and attention.

A boy watering flowers ▶

Fact 187

Weeds are unwelcome plants that grow in gardens and take water and nutrients from the soil. Gardeners should pull out weeds regularly to keep their garden plants healthy and strong.

◀ *Weeding a garden*

Vegetable

Fact 188

Vegetables are the parts of plants that we can eat! Lettuce is one plant's leaves, celery is another's stem and broccoli is a flower. Vegetables are healthy foods that are full of vitamins and nutrients.

Vegetable cart in front of a greengrocer's shop ▼

Fact 189

Not all vegetables are green. Many come in bright colours, such as pink radishes, orange pumpkins, yellow squashes and purple aubergines.

◀ Radishes

Fact 190

Carrots are crunchy orange vegetables that are good for your eyes. If you eat plenty of carrots, they can help you to see better!

Carrots ▶

Fact 191

The tomato is actually a fruit! Scientifically speaking, it has all the characteristics of a fruit. But because the tomato is often used as a vegetable and is not sweet like most fruits, many people consider the tomato a vegetable.

◀ Tomatoes

Fruit

Fact 192

A fruit is a part of a plant we can eat that contains seeds. Some fruits have several seeds, while others have one large seed that can be found inside their stone or pip.

Freshly ripened peaches ▼

Fact 193

Fruits can be soft and sweet like bananas, tart and crispy like apples or even sour and juicy like lemons.

◀ *Mixed berries*

Glass of lemonade ▶

Fact 194

Fruits contain lots of vitamins and minerals. Many drinks are made with fruit, including lemonade, fruit squash, grape juice, orange juice and apple juice.

▼ *Granny Smith apple*

Fact 195

There are more than 7,000 types of apple. One is even named after a grandma. Maria Anne Smith, an Australian grandmother, was the first person to grow the type of apple called a Granny Smith!

Houses made from mud ▶

Mobius Arch, Alabama, USA ▲

Land

Land, the solid part of Earth's surface, is all around us. Whether as big as a mountain or as small as a garden, all land is made of the same things: rock, sand and soil!

Who lives in the land?

Certain animals live in the land. For example, bats live in caves and prairie dogs live inside underground burrows.

Prairie dog ▶

Uses for land

Most people use elements of land – such as stone, clay and soil – to build their homes.

We're digging underground for hidden treasure!

What grows from the land?

A lot of the food we eat grows from the land. Farmers grow fruit trees in their orchards and anyone can grow vegetables in their garden.

Orange grove ▶

113

Rock

Fact 196

Rocks are made up of minerals, which are tiny grains of crystals or metals. They form when minerals are pressed together under extreme pressure or heat.

I'm the king of Pride Rock.

Multicoloured stones ▼

Fact 197

Rocks can be small, such as the tiny pebbles you find in a stream, or as big as a mountain. Some rocks are grainy and dull and others are shiny and sparkly.

◀ *Balancing stones*

Fact 198

People use rocks to build walls, walkways, houses and many other kinds of buildings. Rock is a good material to build with, because it is so heavy and strong.

The Alamo in San Antonio, Texas, USA ▶

Fact 199

While many rocks are rough and jagged, you'll find the smoothest rocks in oceans, streams and rivers, where water is constantly running over them and rounding their rough edges.

◀ *Nightcap National Park in Australia*

115

Soil

Fact 200 Soil is another important part of land. It's made from a mixture of bits of rocks and decayed plants. Soil covers much of the Earth's surface.

Just as I suspected: when soil gets wet, it turns to mud!

Sprouts growing from the soil ▼

Fact 201

Plants need soil to help them stand up tall and strong and to keep their roots safe. Soil also provides the nutrients and water that help plants grow.

◀ *A ploughed field prepared for new planting*

Fact 202

Clay is a special kind of soil. It's smooth, moist and easy to shape into pottery. Once the pottery is baked in a hot oven, it hardens and can be used as vases, plates and cups.

Potter decorating a spinning pot ▶

Fact 203

Loam is a gritty, sticky soil that forms in puddles. Certain birds, called swallows, search for puddles and collect loam from them. Then the swallows use the loam as 'glue' for building their nests.

◀ *Four young swallows in a nest*

Shell

Shells are the exterior skeletons of a group of soft-bodied animals called molluscs.

I love to collect pretty shells!

A variety of seashells ▼

Fact 205

Shells are very important to the molluscs inside them, giving them protection and sometimes camouflage from their enemies.

◀ *Clamshell*

Fact 206

Shell shapes have different purposes. Cone-shaped shells are good for tunnelling underground, smooth, spiral shells glide through wet, heavy sand and ridged shells help anchor molluscs to the ocean floor.

Seashell ▶

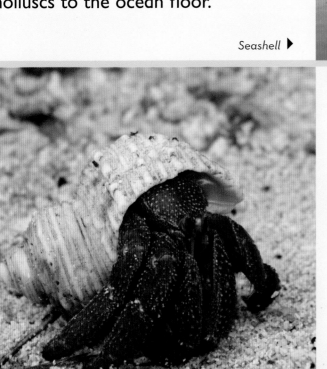

Fact 207

A shell grows as the animal living inside it grows. Once the animal dies, the shell stops growing.

◀ *Hermit crabs borrow the shells of dead molluscs*

Cave

Wow, what a cool cave!

Fact 208
Caves are natural openings in rocky sides of hills or cliffs. All caves are damp and dark. Many are deep enough to have waterfalls and lakes inside them.

Sea caves, Cape Greco, Cyprus ▼

Fact 209

Long ago, people lived in caves. They drew pictures about their lives on the cave walls.

◀ *Bushmen paintings and rock art*

Fact 210

Inside caves, a mixture of water and rock minerals constantly drips from the ceiling – when these drips dry up, the minerals harden into rock formations that look like icicles! They're called stalactites.

Cave with stalactites ▶

Fact 211

Some animals live inside caves. During the day, hundreds of bats sleep close together in the same cave, hanging from the cave ceiling by their feet!

◀ *Group of bats in an underground cave*

Mountain

Fact 212

Mountains, which are made of rock and soil, stand tall above the rest of the land. It takes millions of years for mountains to form. They are still forming all over the world!

The Rocky Mountains, USA, at sunrise ▼

Fact 213

Mountains are home to many animals. Wild goats climb the rocks, mountain lions hunt for animals and eagles soar over the mountaintops, building their large nests along cliffs.

◀ *Mountain goat with kid*

Fact 214

Many people enjoy exploring mountains. In winter, it's fun to ski down snowy mountain slopes. In summer, people enjoy camping and hiking on mountain trails.

Skiing ▶

Fact 215

The top of a mountain, or peak, is its coldest spot. Often you'll see snow on mountain peaks, even in the middle of summer! The highest mountain peaks do not have any plants or trees growing on them.

◀ *Himalayas, Nepal*

Volcano

Fact 216

A volcano is a mountain that forms around a hole, or vent, in the ground. This hole is so deep that it connects to the hot liquid rock that's far below the Earth's surface!

Smokin' hot!

Volcanic eruption ▼

Fact 217

When enough pressure builds up, the hot liquid rock bursts up and explodes through the top of the volcano. This liquid rock is called lava.

◄ *Volcanic eruption*

Fact 218

Lava is a very hot liquid that can reach temperatures of up to around 1,200 degrees Celcius! The word 'volcano' comes from the name of the Roman god of fire, Vulcan.

Lava flowing ▶

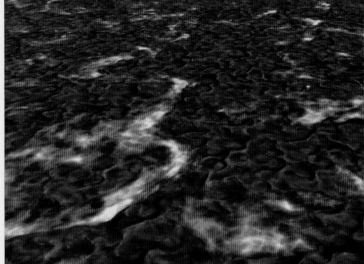

Fact 219

The largest volcano on Earth is Hawaii's Mauna Loa. It rises almost 10 kilometres from the sea floor. However, the largest volcano in our solar system is Olympus Mons on the planet Mars. It is about 27 kilometres high!

◄ *Mauna Loa volcano, Hawaii, USA*

Gold

Gold is a shiny, yellow metal that is relatively soft compared to other metals. This means it can be shaped into money, jewellery, statues and even fillings for teeth!

I love finding lost things that are made of gold!

Gold bars ▼

Fact 221

When people think of gold, they often think of riches and wealth. But did you know that gold is actually a mineral that's found underground?

◄ *Gold running through rock*

Fact 222

After gold is mined – dug out of the ground – it is usually melted down. Once melted, it can be shaped into beautiful jewellery, watches or other items.

Pieces of gold ▶

Fact 223

Gold is a rare metal, which means it's hard to find. Yellow gold is very special, because it's the only metal that doesn't rust or change colour over time.

◄ *Gold chains and necklaces*

Polar bear in the Arctic ▶

Crab underwater ▲

Habitats

Habitats are specific environments where plants and animals with similar needs live.

What are habitats like?

Habitats can be cold and icy, hot and dry, or damp and rainy. Some habitats are under the water and some are underground.

Gorilla in the grasslands ▶

What are habitats?

A habitat contains everything a group of plants and animals needs to survive: just the right amount of light, air, water, soil, food and shelter.

My habitat is Monstropolis!

What lives in a habitat?

Certain plants and animals are suited to live in their habitats. For example, camels and cactus plants need very little water to survive, so they're suited to living in the hot, dry desert.

Camels in the desert ▼

Earth · Habitats

What are habitats?

A habitat contains everything a group of plants and animals needs to survive: just the right amount of light, air, water, soil, food and shelter.

My habitat is Monstropolis!

What lives in a habitat?

Certain plants and animals are suited to live in their habitats. For example, camels and cactus plants need very little water to survive, so they're suited to living in the hot, dry desert.

Camels in the desert ▼

129

Tropical rainforest

Fact 224 Tropical rainforests are warm, wet forests that are home to millions of different plants and animals. They are very important to humans, because rainforests create most of the Earth's oxygen, which we need to breathe.

Canopy of the Amazon rainforest ▼

Fact 225

Tropical rainforests are found in Africa, Asia, Australia, India and South America. Some rainforests get more than 250 centimetres of rain each year.

◀ *Gaudy leaf tree frog*

Natural moss growing on rocks ▶

Fact 226

Trees in a tropical rainforest are so leafy and grow so close together, that rain falling on treetops can take about 10 minutes to finally reach the forest floor!

Fact 227

Australian rainforests are filled with unique flowers. About 80 per cent of the flowers found in Australian rainforests cannot be found anywhere else on Earth.

◀ *Grevillea blooming in an Australian rainforest*

African savannah

Fact 228 Grasslands in Africa are called savannahs. Savannahs are covered with tall grasses, with hardy trees dotting the landscape.

Lots of animals live in savannahs!

African zebras ▼

132

Fact 229

Although they have a rainy season lasting several months, savannahs are hot and dry the rest of the year.

◀ *African elephant*

Fact 230

Some savannah grass grows as tall as a grown-up human! Grass is an important food for animals such as zebras and antelopes, who spend their days grazing.

Antelope ▶

Fact 231

The African savannah is home to the world's fastest land animal (the cheetah), the world's largest land animal (the African elephant) and the world's tallest animal (the giraffe)!

◀ *Cheetah*

133

Australian grassland

Fact 232 The Australian grasslands are full of wildlife and plants and dotted with farms, called 'stations'.

Sheep grazing on a farm in New South Wales, Australia ▼

Fact 233

The animals living in the Australian grasslands have adapted to the dry, windy conditions. Emus, kangaroos, wallabies and wombats all do well in this environment.

◀ *Wallaby in a grassy paddock*

Fact 234

Kangaroo paw is a beautiful plant found in Australia's grasslands. Its flowers look like little kangaroo paws! Birds called honeyeaters drink the nectar from this plant's flowers.

Yellow kangaroo paw ▶

◀ *Golden dingo pups*

Fact 235

Dingoes are wild dogs that live in the grasslands of Australia. They live in family groups called packs, which might have between 3 and 12 dogs. At night, packs hunt for rats, rabbits, lizards, birds and kangaroos.

Desert

Fact 236 Deserts are the driest places on Earth. It rarely rains, so desert plants and animals – such as cactus plants and camels – must be able to survive with very little water.

I'd love to explore the desert!

Large camels in the desert ▼

Fact 237

When it does rain in the desert, a storm may last a few hours, and then it might not rain again for many months – or even years! A few weeks after it rains, bright wildflowers sometimes appear in the desert.

◀ *Small desert flower*

A fennec, or desert, fox asleep against a rock ▶

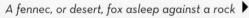

Fact 238

Although a few deserts are cold during the day, most are very hot and dry. During daylight, many animals escape the heat by tunnelling underground. At night, however, even the hottest deserts can drop to freezing temperatures.

Fact 239

Africa's Sahara desert is the largest desert in the world. It covers over nine million square kilometres!

◀ *Sahara desert landscape*

Fun facts!

The friends from *The Lion King* have been finding out all sorts of cool facts about the unique animal habitats around the world. Read what they've discovered about animal homes!

Barn

FACT 240 Some farm animals, such as horses and pigs, sleep in large buildings called barns. Instead of bedrooms, the barn has special areas called stalls where the animals sleep. Most farm animals sleep on beds of straw.

FACT 241 On the farm, chickens often live in buildings called coops. Chicken coops have perches and rows of nesting boxes where the chickens can lay their eggs.

Web

FACT 246 Spiders spin beautiful webs using a special silk that shoots from their bodies. If you've ever touched a web, you know that parts of it can stick to your fingers.

FACT 247 Spiders catch insects in their webs to eat. Spiders never get stuck in their own webs thanks to the special claws that they have on their feet!

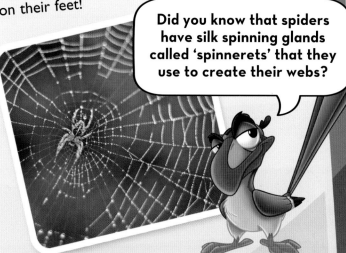

Nest

FACT 242 Many birds live in homes called nests. Nests, which are shaped like cups or bowls, are cosy places for birds to lay their eggs and raise their babies.

FACT 243 A mother bird flies away from the nest to find worms and insects to feed her babies. Baby birds live in their nests until they are old enough to fly on their own.

Beehive

FACT 248 Honeybees live in homes called hives, which are made up of little six-sided tubes or 'rooms' called combs. Thousands of honeybees can live together in one hive.

FACT 249 Once bees collect nectar from flowers, they store the nectar in the combs where it changes into honey. This supply of honey is what the bees will live on in winter.

Burrow

FACT 244 Many animals, such as moles, rabbits, skunks, snakes and toads, live in holes or tunnels in the ground. These holes are called burrows.

FACT 245 To make their tunnels, earthworms eat the soil as they burrow into it! Earthworms live in moist soil, often under rocks and logs.

Index

141

nds Lakes Summer Sun Snal

Water Amphibi Walrus

Learn P ig Bat strich

Stream Zebra

Soil Tree Ostrich

Caterpillar

Autumn Cat Dog Mammal

B Forest

Bee Egg Bir Reptile